PRESS

*

TO
ENGAGE

PRESS

TO
ENGAGE

KAREN KHAW

PARTRIDGE
A Penguin Random House Company

To order additional copies of this book, contact
Toll Free 800 101 2657 (Singapore)
Toll Free 1 800 81 7340 (Malaysia)
orders.singapore@partridgepublishing.com

www.partridgepublishing.com/singapore

The sub-topics

About the Author

Karen Khaw is a communications and marketing professional with cross-industry exposure and zest for life. Born in Malaysia, Karen was brought up in Australia and now working while living in Hong Kong. With a natural ability to adapt and creatively-minded, Karen loves nurturing young talents especially in the areas of marketing, communication and employee engagement. Her first book is a testimony of one of her passions – demystifying the topic of employee engagement. Karen has over 15 years Asia Pacific experience in advising, leading and realizing marketing as well as communication programs in both financial and professional services. Having worked for Westpac and the Commonwealth Bank of Australia in Sydney, Karen moved to Hong Kong to join Baker

& McKenzie in 2006. Having spent four years at Societe Generale Corporate & Investment Banking as a Corporate Communications professional, Karen joined BNY Mellon in Hong Kong in 2011.

PREFACE

A **promise is a promise.** In fact, this book in itself is a promise to my dear friend – Mukta Arya. A Conversation at a bar near Hong Kong's Lan Kwai Fong (a rare but memorable occasion) on the topic of new year's resolutions is now finally a reality.

As children, I am sure many of us would have been told by your elders, "it is a promise" and often followed by the "finger-wrapping" ritual to lock in the agreement. The next thing the child will then expect is usually that the elder would keep that promise – whatever that might be or at least tell them when it would be realized, if it is not now.

Well, it is not that different in business. If a company makes a promise to their employees, be it through the interview or annual review conversation, their employees would expect the company to keep that promise or at least give a reason why it would not be kept. Ever heard of the praise "over-promise, under-deliver"..... precisely my point. The promises made to employees are very important and relevant when it comes to ensuring strong employee engagement.

A promise is certainly a promise. Employee engagement is not just words but rather actions. While I am not a qualified psychologist with a relevant background on understanding the human mind, I have experience of this subject from my many years as both a manager and an employee. The other motivation being I enjoy seeing others succeed in making a 'real' change to the way they approach engaging their employees.

Promises are made to be broken. This is not a contradiction to the earlier points made but a reality. After all we do live in the 'real' world where situations change, things do go wrong, people's situation change and so on. It is how you handle the situation when you have to break your promise that really matters.

I hope this book gives a broader view to the meaning of employee engagement to those interested.

Although engagement can seem complex and often an intimidating topic to tackle, it is part and parcel of running a sustainable organization.

The views and ideas expressed in this book are strictly my personal opinion and all names references are fictional. This book is designed to be a light read for anyone who is curious or interested in the topic of engagement.

This book is an encouraged outcome of a true and engaging friend who is an author herself having published two meaningful sharing of her poems collection since she moved to Hong Kong. Mukta Arya, this book is dedicated to you for being the 'driver' and my 'friend of choice'.

Special thanks to a list of amazing managers who have been great mentors in my life, and still are – guiding, inspiring and encouraging throughout – John Powell, Mark Mulligan, Lisa Bremner, Paul Rickard, Michael Blomfield, Ian Saines, Laurent Tison, Dominique Henzell, Dan Smith, Dean Stephan, Amy Pershing and of course, Sally Savory, who made it possible.

Thank you to Kate Henley, for ensuring I push my limits to achieve the best I can. Special dedication to my amazingly talented husband Dylan and beautiful daughter Sophie, both of whom have taught me so much and made me realize the beauty of a balanced life. To the family who crafted me into who I am today - Mom, Dad, Jo, Dave, Alicia, Sebastian, Chris and Terry - this is for you too.

As much as I would get criticized for saying it "have a great read!".

Engagement is not a one-off....................................

ENGAGEMENT IS NOT A ONE-OFF...

Engagement is a lifecycle

This book is not in any way a manual or a step-by-step guide to improving employee engagement. It is a perspective on what employee engagement might mean, and in my experience, what might be meaningful to employees. In fact, there is no step-by-step guide that will perfectly set out how to create engagement - unless you do not employ people in your business. If you rely on human beings to help run your business (no matter if it is one person or cast of thousands), then you need to pay attention to employee engagement.

A business without engagement from your employees is equivalent to an empty house with no lights – there is no life, no energy hence not inviting.

So this book is about turning the lights on, making the workplace an inviting space, and engaging your team in many different ways at each stage of their career. Engagement is not a 'one off' activity. It is an enduring process that is more important than you may think.

Yet so often, employee engagement is sometimes just another item on the corporate agenda, a box that just needs to be ticked. Sometimes it is developed as a one-off management process, something that needs to be completed as an agenda item, but is then not fully developed or nurtured. Or worse, launched with fanfare and then left to languish.

Sometimes companies strive to achieve 'Employer of Choice' status – to be chosen and preferred by most employees. Such awards become an accolade for the company and its image.

Or perhaps the **employee** engagement survey result is below the benchmark of peers. Suddenly **employee** engagement becomes the management team's top priority, as no company wants to be last in the competition and image stakes.

What is also often clear is that there is no simple explanation people can themselves offer up about the meaning of **'employee engagement'**. Most, if they could, will talk about social events and outings. Certainly such events might form part of a employee engagement plan, but is this all there is? There is so much more, at many levels and layers.

Think of engagement on 3 levels. For those visual thinkers, imagine an asterisk (✻).

1) Engagement *through* the employee lifecycle (horizontal line -): from the moment people join the company, to when they depart the company. Importantly also, it covers the employees returning to the company.

2) Engagement *top-down vs bottom*-up (vertical line |): engagement within the team and its managers.

3) Engagement *across* the company (diagonal lines on both sides X): engagement with others in the company that people do not have a direct relationship with. For example, the receptionist in Hong Kong and the Chief

Operating Officer of the company based in London who have never ever met. Engagement is needed at each and every stage of the employee lifecycle.

Perhaps many of you by now are asking the reason for reading on?

Why should we need to spend time on **employee** engagement - besides the fact that it is in most senior management's annual performance objectives or is a company mandate?

What is clear is that keeping your employees happy equals keeping your clients happy, ensuring the sustainability of your business.

The best way to visualize why we should engage employees is to imagine the alternative. Imagine that employee engagement is not given any attention at all. Here is a simple scenario, involving the fictitious ABC Call Centre, to solidify the point made.

NOT ENGAGING......

John, team leader at ABC call centre based in Singapore has two members in his team, Ling and Masaki. Ling has been with the firm for five years. Masaki has been with the firm for 2 days. John has been with the firm for 20 years and has made numerous recommendations over that time regarding improvements to the call centre.

A Client calls about a complaint, which was answered by Ling. She has been working long hours in the call centre and has been told by John that there is no chance for a promotion for at least another 3 to 5 years. Ling could not care less about the client's complaint nor does she have any incentive to fix the client's problem. The Client asks to speak with John.

Ever since he took on his team leader role 5 years ago, John has wanted to visit the headquarters in Shanghai to review the centre and to make some improvements regarding the client experience at the call centre. John picks the phone up and listens for 5 seconds.

He apologizes as he has done for the last 40 complaints, as the basic issues at the call centre will remain until he gets to do something about it. The Client, disgusted, ends the call and takes business elsewhere. The client experience is completely negative.

Ling and John continued their day, counting the minutes before they could get out of the door.

Masaki, new to Singapore, has yet to get a chance to speak a word to anyone in his team since he arrived 2 days ago.

What is the level of employee engagement here?

And what could have been done to improve it?

Engagement throughout the employee lifecycle.....

ENGAGEMENT THROUGHOUT THE EMPLOYEE LIFECYCLE (-)...

The moments of truth – the horizontal line.

You may have heard of "the lifecycle" concept in marketing. The same applies to employee engagement only here it unfolds over several stages. The first stage is certainly the moment an employee joins the company, whether it is the induction or new joiners session with many others or the office tour with a direct manager.

This is where expectations developed during the earlier interviews should match with reality. If it does not match, then it is highly likely the employee will not be there any longer than past the probation - either by choice or at the company's choice.

From a management viewpoint, this is the first moment to communicate their first promise to enthusiastic employees. The engagement level is usually near the highest at this point.

Our employee has just given up another relationship (company) to come work **with you** - not withstanding the many interviews, compliance mechanisms and checks they have already endured. So they are keen. Just try to count the time and money as well as work-hours already spent overall, simply to get the new employee to step into the office on day one. That is already a large investment. So, if **your** promise does not resonate with the new joiner, then the work gets harder from here on. It is important to be realistic, do not over-promise. State the expectations and your company's proposition simply as it is.

I can share a personal example that until today still stays in my books as the best new joiner speech I have ever heard and I would certainly return to work for this company at any time – making my point. It is because the company set the right tone and was realistic about the role as well as expectations.

THE REALITY CHECK

I shifted from working in foreign exchange to online stockbroking not long after I graduated from University, many years ago. That was during the birth of online stockbroking and when the internet was still an unknown. The client service head of the online stockbroking spoke to a group of new joiners about the reality of working for the firm. Quote "if you think you are a stockbroker and have joined a stockbroking firm, then please leave now. You are, if you get through your probation, a client service specialist working for an online stockbroker." If you managed to impress the new joiners during the induction section then you have yourself enthusiastic advocates for at least the next few months.

What is your new joiners pitch?

How realistic is it?

Will the employee be able to recognize this proposition in three months time?

The next milestone or second moment of truth is the probation deadline - as it is the moment we see if the promise still matches reality. It is either go straight pass 'GO' or 'thank you very much, it has been nice working with you'.

If you think about it, the performance of the individual is already evident at that moment in time. If they were just average at the time of the probation deadline, do not expect a sudden spike in performance as soon as you confirm their permanent employment. Improvement is unlikely, unless you are prepared to invest significant amount of time and effort in the individual. It may not necessarily mean the person is not capable - but more likely the wrong fit. Of course, there are exceptions, especially when viewed from an employee's perspective but once again, be realistic

The third moment of truth is when the individual reaches their one-year anniversary. They might fairly ask, "Will my boss remember my work anniversary?".

Employer's should ask the question including, "Do we have an automatic trigger either in the system or in our

calendar to remind us of this important milestone?".
Also, "What are we doing to recognize this occasion?".

Usually, given it is the first year, the expectation of the
employee is often much lower, hence a simple personal
congratulations will do the trick. This can be face-to-
face, a simple message or even an SMS.

Anyone forgetting this milestone will need to double
their effort the next year to convince the individual
that they are appreciated. After all, we are all
human, with feelings and seek recognition as well as
acknowledgement.

Many companies now have some sort of service
anniversary recognition program in place, especially for
milestone years such as 5, 10 or 15 years and so on. There
is therefore some expectation that these milestones be
recognized and thought should be given as to how these
milestones will be acknowledged. A handshake? The
old gold watch or pen? A plaque or certificate?

Or being recognized in front of all your colleagues? It
depends on the type of values your company wishes
to display. Tight on clients and splashes on employees?
Length of service is secondary to performance? Every

year matters? Perhaps review your company culture and strategy to find the answer. There is no model answer, just what suits your company.

Apart from milestone years, the life events of an employee should also be taken into consideration when attempting engagement of employees.

Managing Life Events

Not unlike our clients, our employees themselves live life and go through various stages and events including engagement, marriage, child birth, loss, new home, health issues and so on. While it is not the employer's responsibility to be aware of each life event of the employee (or managers will be working way more than 24/7), it is an aspect that needs to be considered when looking at the company's employee engagement strategy and plan, in order to ensure the necessary support program is available.

This is where the Human Resources linkage comes into the picture. Is the benefits structure supporting these life events? Are managers trained to handle these or at least know who to contact?

Imagine a manager who tells an employee to keep working late hours when the employee has explained that they have just had a new-born baby. The suggestion is not that employers should all become soft-hearted, but rather that being considerate is being human.

If there is an important deal that absolutely requires the presence of a new parent in order to reach completion, then the manager should review the business continuity aspect of his or her team. No manager can afford to think that they will always have a full team operating at full capacity. If we do not expect all computers to be perfect, then why should we think the same of human beings?

There should ideally be a simple set of steps an employee should take when there comes a need to be excused. For example, having the ability to set the "out of office" remotely, or possibly the ability to have it activated by others. Or enabling access to a communication device for all employees to get in touch urgently if required. This is to ensure the safety of the employee. Some companies also have a policy banning other employees from contacting the employee who is on leave (regardless of type of leave).

The employee-employer relationship is often not that different to that of our personal relationships. It does draw on a certain level of trust.

MINING EMPLOYEE TRENDS

Let's step aside for a short moment. In database marketing, data mining is common to identify trends to enable better targeting. For example, who are the best targets for a new home loan? Clients who have just been married and have asked to change their status? A female client who has recently changed her surname to a married name? Significant savings status? These are triggers that may indicate a higher than normal likeliness for the client to be seeking a new home, and therefore possibly a home loan. So applying this in the workplace: Have employees been recently married? Do they have elderly parents? Specials needs children? A new baby? Are they studying for exams? Have they been with the company for 5, 7, or 10 years? More?

How many companies have this type of system in place for monitoring their employees' lifecycle and longevity in a formalized way?

Does this bottom-up approach feed back to the top line high potential or top performers retention plan?

The Seven Year Itch

We have often talked about 'the seven year itch" when it comes to personal relationships. The seven year itch often exists in the employee-employer relationships too. Employees often see five years as a milestone - but have a significantly higher expectation of the employer when it gets to the seventh year. At this seventh year stage, it is crucial (if this was not already done at the five year mark) to find time to review the performance and potential of the employee and devise an appropriate plan. We have all heard the statement that it costs much more to recruit a new employee than to retain one. So if you have a slight indication that the employee who has worked for seven years may leave the company if their expectations are not met, then why wouldn't you be proactive in starting the conversation? Common sense tells us that an employee who has lasted seven years would tell the truth regarding how they feel about the company. After all, seven years is not a short amount of time, it is an investment.

Employees are human beings so they need to feel valued which can come in different forms:

- As surprising as it may seem, remuneration although a factor, is not the only aspect an employee values. This is especially true if they have been in the company for more than seven years.
- Relaying the benefit of their seven years' experience to others in the company may make them feel important. Consider these employees as good candidates to speak at the next new joiners session.
- Promotion is important of course - but that could also be vertical to other departments - or across the organization, such as a transfer to another location. Secondments also can often re-ignite employees' energy and make them feel valued.
- Conduct a conversation to assess the employees possibly renewed expectations - they may be wanting a short career break or sabbatical. Possibly exposure to help in a new project. They may even value the offer to access an independent corporate coach.

> In short, be proactive and do not wait for the employee to come to you to ask. If there are performance issues, well, then perhaps you should ask why it has taken seven years to notice.

Having worked in a law firm, I certainly have a good appreciation of the professional-client relationship. As part of every law firm pitch, you will often find a section outlining 'why you should choose our law firm as your preferred counselor'. Depending on the client, sometimes access to secondees (usually an associate) from the law firm may be listed as a client benefit. Apart from professional services firms, do other companies provide similar benefits to their clients?

Of course, things sometimes may not work out the way you want it to. Factoring in headhunters, personal choices and the unexpected, there may be cases where even the most engaged and loyal employee may one day leave you the exit note you never wish to receive as a manager. Many may consider that to be the last of the engagement journey of an employee - but not in my book.

This employee has friends, families and a memory too. While it is not the employer's role to mind-read and keep track of what causes an employee exodus, no one should rule out this employee returning - especially when it is a life event that has caused them to leave the company. Remember, a returning and engaged employee is near equivalent to retaining an existing employee – lower cost, engaged and most likely already your ambassador

---

Ask yourself: which company have you left that you would be happy to work for again, if they made you a return offer tomorrow? If you are serious about investing in engaging your employees then this should be your company's name. The bottom line to the employee engagement lifecycle – think about employees as you would your clients.

Be proactive in managing your employees' expectations throughout all their milestones in the company. Employee loyalty programs, acknowledgements, employee congratulations for anniversaries and lifecycle, expectations and promotions discussions - give your employees reasons to stick with you.

Engagement top-down vs bottom-up......................

ENGAGEMENT
TOP-DOWN VS BOTTOM-UP (+)...

Partnership and Communication

Top-down vs bottom-up - this is often used in managed funds to explain the management approach or more commonly, as the way a message is being cascaded in an organization. There is no mystery to this second axis to employee engagement, in that investment in this topic should start from the top and be supported by the entire employee base. Communication plays a crucial role in ensuring this axis meets its balance. The other partnering theme is training and development. All through this axis, employees should ideally be speaking the same language and acting out the same messages.

Start where you are. Employee engagement is not just the responsibility of a manager and team leader but of all of us. It is often the case that employee engagement is within the performance objective of a manager but is seldom in every employee's performance plan. Is employee engagement necessarily the responsibility of top management? Or should employees also be responsible for employee engagement?

Many companies have started to realize the benefit of encouraging both bottom-up as well as top-down responsibilities for employee engagement. The bottom-up perspective actually started many years ago – remember those social clubs? The occasional team building or social activities that you now get invited to? Such activities are usually organized by a representative group of employees who are passionate about arranging activities that are fun for employees. These early social club events have evolved over time to become more inclusive programs that are now continuously designed and implemented in order to help engage employees more fully across all levels, areas, locations and background.

Of course you will always get your usual suspects, employees who attend every event ever held, as well as your 'invisibles' who you will never see, no matter what type of event. Nonetheless, such activities were at least partly seen as employee engagement. Isn't the intention of such activities to make employees loyal and happy about working for the company?

As we have progressed on the employee engagement journey, we have found that 'fun at work' or even more engaging community activities are not the only factors that contribute towards an engaged employee base. In addition to employee fun days and monetary benefits, employees demand other meaningful benefits, such as training, professional development, recognition by management and team, mentoring, appropriate resources, and an updated understanding of the direction and values of the company to ensure that it aligns with their career plans and personal values.

From my years working for global companies, the employee groups concept is not new but quite often these groups are challenged in terms of their measurable value and exact role. The idea is always great but the process of how they should operate over the long term is often blurry and dependent on how they are led or managed at that time. While I do not disagree that the employee engagement program should be kept fluid given the volatile working environment we currently operate in, some basic structure is required to ensure this is not just another 'tick the box' item. Perhaps, more about the structure in my next book.

I am certainly not alluding to a list of metrics that should be put in place which will require a metrics expert to decipher - but rather a good enough framework with clear focus, objectives, timeline and strategy.

One thing that is crucial in maintaining a sustainable employee engagement program is to be realistic. Do not over-promise and under or never deliver. That is by far the worst mistake that can be made if you are aiming for employer of choice status. Furthermore, employees want you to be realistic when dealing with their engagement at work.

NON-DELIVERY DISAPPOINTS

To draw another analogy, take the example of a young 4-year old child who was promised by his mother that he would receive a candy if he behaves himself. After being a well-behaved child the whole day, when the child next saw his mother, he asked for the candy that was promised.

> *His mother did not get the chance to get him the candy and subsequently promised that she will give him a packet of candies tomorrow. The child continues to behave well the next day longing waiting near the door for his mother to return with the packet of candies, then to find out that she had once again forgotten. His mother has now increased the stakes by making another promise to give the child two large packets of candies tomorrow when she returns. When the child continues to behave for the third day expecting to get the two large packets of candies....and so on. Imagine being the child (replace with an employee) keeping to your promise of behaving well but never receiving any part of what you were promised by the mother (replace with the company).*

Hence it is important to set out what is achievable in terms of realistic goals and actions that can be used to improve engagement. It is not a "big words" competition but rather a challenge - what exactly are you going to do to meet your engagement goals? It is not 'transform the company into employer of choice within 24 hours' but rather 'launch a new intranet site to host all documents that will make employees' lives better by no later than end of March this year'. Keep it simple. That is by far the only way to really start moving the needle, when it comes to improving employee engagement.

Engagement across the company..................

ENGAGEMENT ACROSS
THE COMPANY (*)...

Start with those around you.

The phrase "across the company" (the diagonal lines) is likely to worry most employees and managers. A big job, lots of barriers, a long time, how do I get everyone across the whole company to behave the same way? Where do I start? Start right where you can. With yourself and those around you. Achieving engagement across the company is not about ensuring every employee is a replica of another employee, as this will only lead to a company with no diversity. Engagement across the company is about consistency, collaboration of a diverse employee base and continuity.

The vision here is to get to a point where regardless of whether you speak with the graduate trainee in the New York office, the senior manager in the Seoul office or the analyst in the Poland office, they will say the exact same thing about the company's direction, culture and intentions.

I cannot avoid returning to the concept of the 'key message', given my background. The vision is this: what is 'that' one, unprompted, common response that each employee would say about the company? Looking for examples or do not know what I mean?

This is easy to get a sense of today given the availability of the web and social platforms.

WHO ARE WE?

Try this for an example. Type in a company's name and the word 'blog' or 'review'. A few blogs or chats will usually show up – read through what people say about the company and you will shortly get a flavor or a common theme. That theme is 'that thing they are saying about the company'. That theme will give you a sense of where you are in your employee engagement journey. Yes, just a sense of course as it is not statistically proven after all - so do not take it personally.

Have you reviewed your company's image on the blogsphere?

What would you want the one unprompted response to be?

So, if you have yet to think about engagement of your employees or the one and only employee you hire, then start the journey now, as better late than never.

Employee Engagement is not a rush job

Pushing too many initiatives to drive employee engagement at the same time can be detrimental to the success of any employee engagement program. You can of course do so if you have true commitment and ownership for each initiative. Sustainability surpasses quantity. If you decide on an initiative then follow through all the way or it should be pushed down the priority list. Introduce a few key initiatives and deliver them really well. Do you expect your employees to hand in 'half-baked' solutions to your clients? Well, they may if they themselves are receiving 'half-baked' engagement initiatives. No prizes for creating the longest list of employee engagement initiatives but a definite win if you have all your employees standing by your brand (how about wearing your company's brand on an umbrella or sports bag on the weekend).

The purpose of this book, as stated in the preface, is to give another perspective to viewing employee engagement rather than as a step-by-step guide. All content and ideas are based solely on my personal opinion and names used are fictitious. The topic is just as important from an employee's perspective – to understand what your employers are trying to do to assist engagement. My concluding personal views – it is a two -way street requiring engagement, partnership and involvement from both sides to function. The more you put in, the more you get back overtime – both ways that is – as an employer as well as an employee.

It is fine to not know how to improve engagement, as it should be done with your employees, so work together to derive the solutions.

Finally, if you have not started your engagement journey then start now - press * to engage.